THE COMEDY OF DESIRE

THE COMEDY OF DESIRE

❊

NILS PETERSON

DRAWINGS BY RITA SHUMAKER

BLUE SOFA PRESS

Edited by Andrew Dick and Robert Bly.

Graphic design by Cats Pajamas Inc. and Philip Lang.

Cover art by Henri Matisse, "Back," lithograph,
with permission of The Metropolitan Museum of Art,
Rogers Fund, 1921. (21.97.6)

Back cover photo by Conrad Rushing.

ISBN 0-9638722-0-6

Library of Congress Catalog Card Number 93-74913

The Comedy of Desire is the first volume in a series from Blue Sofa Press:
a cooperative effort, operated and funded by artists and writers.
Blue Sofa was created to make available some of the work that has grown out
of the Great Mother and New Father Conference, now in its nineteenth year.

Grateful acknowledgement is made to the editors of the following magazines
in which versions of some of these poems were printed earlier:
Painted Bride Quarterly, Mildred, San Jose Studies, The Men's Journal, Reed,
Clinton Street Quarterly, Sonoma Review, and Centrepiece.

Special thanks to the San Jose Center for Poetry and Literature,
and to Nick Zachreson of Blackwell's Press
for the publication of two broadsides
which contain several of
these poems.

BLUE SOFA PRESS
Distributed by Ally Press
524 Orleans Street, Saint Paul, Minnesota 55104

Printed in Canada

Dedicated to the many women
who helped me understand
something of the feminine
but particularly to
Judith, Erika and Cecily.

When the best is gone,
I know that other things are not of consequence.
The heart wants what it wants,
Or else it does not care.

Emily Dickinson

COMEDY AND BEAUTY

Nils Peterson is that rare thing in contemporary American poetry, a comic poet who does not diminish the world with his humor. For example, in "An Academic Poem, or A Hero's Life," the Chaucerian comedy is genuinely alive and brisk. The half-maddened wife of a boring professor consoles herself by knitting when she has to listen to a lecture, and occasionally saying aloud, "Freddy, you fool." Nils Peterson's gift for comedy also shows in his willingness to present himself as a gangly, innocent, greedy, utterly incompetent lover.

Some of these poems present the author as fifty years old or so, describing what he sees, visiting, say, Florence, and admiring its street life and Michelangelo's art. But in other pieces, the poem carries us back in a kind of fit of memory to the consciousness of the 20-year-old, who is smitten, who cannot eat or sleep, who cannot believe how marvellous the beautiful and popular girl looks to him. It is an obsession with beauty. This fascination for the charm of the female body seems to have been present even in the sixth grade. The poem "Sometimes You Need to Leave Your History" describes a boy whose desire energy literally leaves his body, is pulled out of it, situating the center of gravity eight or ten feet away in that beautiful sixth-grade girl "whose blouse never quite fit." The boy is not strengthened by his experience of beauty, but isolated and unnerved.

Nils Peterson's subject then in some poems is a passion for the body, a lust for the female, a desire for continuation of the species, and a fascination with "the other," all of which makes a ballroom full of women an extremely confusing and mad place full of hurricanes and tornadoes. And yet his poems make clear that those romantic emotions that impel young men to sing three hours outside the women's dormitory, or go without sleeping for nights on end, are not only experiences of sexual desire. They are also instances of pure longing as intense as a poet's longing for a poem or a saint's longing to be given a sign. In such moments, the man does not want anything "physical;" he wants to know that he is capable of being seen by the warm glory of earthly life. Hafez says in another connection:

> Oh East Wind, take this dust of mine,
> Throw it out to the One Divine,
> So the King of grace and beauty may
> Turn his face and throw one glance our way.

If we change the word "King" here to"Queen," (translation by Walter Stanley) we can sense how much the young man wants to be seen by the Queen of grace and beauty. He longs that she will throw just one glance his way.

The young man who can see light coming under the door of beauty is lucky; if he can't, it's all over with him. He will fall into a serious despair, or give in to the pull of suicide, or fade into some faceless, passionless, neutered existence.

Is all this romantic seeing projection? Is Nils Peterson really seeing a woman, or is it a phantasm, a fragment of mother longing, the "white footfall" Yeats remembers, a bit of Eden, the benevolent side of the Great Mother, the charm of the universe itself, or the first glimpse of his own soul? Well, Marie-Louise von Franz remarks, if we didn't project when young, we'd remain in our own rooms all our life.

A young man or woman ordinarily doesn't ask that question about projection. The mature man or woman does. Nils Peterson recounts in "Once I Went with a Girl Too Beautiful" a dream he had while in London as an adult. In the dream he is back in college "trying to do better," and sees a woman he had loved in his shy way twenty years before. Even now he can only talk politely, so he turns to go. But she calls out, "Look at me." When he doesn't stop, she cries, "LOOK AT ME!" There is something fine in this sequence. The dreamer gives the romantic a rebuke, which the poet records.

Occasionally in these poems the rhythm becomes prosaic or the language too practical. Nils Peterson is not trying to present perfect poems of desire or perfect poems of yearning, but to help us remember with perfection and grace our own confusion during our meetings with the—so-called—divine feminine. The poems have great affection for the feminine, and they are wonderfully patient with human confusion. I also admire the generosity of praise in these poems: the praise of John Logan and his marvellous poetry, the affectionate words for Tomas Tranströmer and his wife Monica, the praise of Denise Levertov, of Abby Niebauer, the poet who died so young, of Naomi Clark, and beyond that the honoring of that wide community of poetry in San Jose of which Nils Peterson has always been such a radiant member.

ROBERT BLY

INVOCATION

In spring when you appear
the hearts of all grow great with longing.

The small bird turns fierce for love,
and heavy-footed farm animals push

against the fences of the warming fields.
So, the shy man leaves his house

throat filled with song. Accept,
O Goddess, these lines whose divine

source you are, for without you, nothing
comes into being beneath the changing moon.

TABLE OF CONTENTS

Once I Went with a Girl Too Beautiful

Once I went with a girl too beautiful
for me. It was a relief not to have to haggle
with the nickels and dimes of my poor heart.
She was too much. I did not even make
a pass, I was that dumb, partly out of my own
nature, but partly having been struck so.
I watched, rather, in awe at the way flesh
transfigures itself by hanging right.
Now and then I would wonder what
is she doing out with me? I had no answer;
so, when she got engaged to the co-captain
of the football team, my hurt was real,
but the ending seemed right, my sense of plot satisfied.

The scene changes. 20 years later. London.
Wife and daughters in California—perhaps lost
to me. I have started reading Jung. Sort of
interested. One night in a dream my beautiful
woman comes back, I again in college trying
to do better. I meet her in the street. We talk
politely, then I start to go. She calls out,
    Look at me,
         but I keep going.
She cries out,
   LOOK AT ME.
       I stop, turn,
and see my old girl reclothed and queenly
the dress of her desiring swirling about
like a summer night when every star,
wanting to be no less than itself, lets
its light full on, and I try, at last,
my absolute best to look at her.

My Lecture on Romanticism

And a spirit in my feet,
Hath led me—who knows how?
To thy chamber-window, Sweet!

P.B. Shelley

It is spring—a hundred years ago
and I am a freshman at a small Kentucky college.
Air is heavy and sweet and heavy and sweet
is the flesh that hangs about the bones whispering.
The witching hour has come and gone—the dark
world lingers bewitched, and Doug, my roommate,
has set off to rescue his girl. Also it is fall
a hundred years from then and I am putting
together a lecture on romanticism for the lumbering
course I teach on the history of everything.

Doug was my second roommate that freshman year,
the first had gone off to the Deke house
with the other football players to butt heads,
drink beer, and date the girls with the biggest
boobs, and Doug was a liar, but maybe there was something
about the blank open naive gullible
faces of Purdom and Klell Napps and me
which drove him to it, which made him tell us,
though he wore glasses and was only a little
less scared and skinny than we that he had been
a forest ranger and a paratrooper, or that
the plain brown wrapper he received
each month in the mail was really hot

stuff conceived in the sewers of Paris for men
ready for mature thrills. *Will they,
can I make them, for God's sake, believe
this?*, I imagine him saying to himself,
looking up over coffee at us who
not believing, yes, believed. Looking
for action in the brown envelope he for once
did not lock in his desk, I discovered
the Charles Atlas course whose dynamic
tensions he later admitted performing in the shower
those mornings he cut class which gave him,
as a matter of fact, much time to practice.
He had a guitar and taught me how to play
the three or four chords of which I'm still
confident, though, as it turned out, the reason
his guitar was out all the time was that
its case, stuck in the back of our closet, hid
his gun collection—two rifles, three
pistols, and what looked like about the right
amount of ammunition to take along
when being dropped behind the lines at Pan-
munjon which we had begun to realize might
happen to us. Anyway, as I assemble
my notes on Blake, Wordsworth, and Keats,
I think of him because in the middle of winter he found
and fell in love with the only girl named Mimi
in all of central Kentucky. Her father
was a refugee too, but from Vienna, not New Jersey
or New York like Doug, my first roommate,
and me, and made his living in some exotic
unKentucky way—breeder of orchids,
or analyst, or tracer of lost persons. She
was a lovely girl, a little stocky, but
the owner of a jeep, a genuine real surplus

army jeep which her father had bought for two
hundred bucks a couple of years before
and in which she would haul our unseatbelted
asses out to the lake in the springtime
by which time she had already said goodbye
to Doug, and Doug, although he slept in our room
and ate occasionally at the cafeteria,
had said goodbye to the school to hang out
with the railroad men who sat all night
long swapping yarns around the greasy
tables of the Coffee Cup Cafe where
a dinner of two pork chops, French
fries, salad, and unlimited coffee
cost eighty five cents. I think
of him now because in that Kentucky
spring—air lovely with lilac, with magnolia,
languorous with the mating of bird, beast, flower,
and upperclassman—he got drunk on the moonshine
that appeared miraculously in old turnip jars
at the dorm, fraternity parties, or the pool halls
that attached limpet-like to the backs of small
restaurants—and set out to rescue
Mimi from "the base durance and contagious prison"
of the Kentucky College for Women, and, arriving
intact across town, rattled that many-
columned splendor with the bassness of his fine deep
voice calling "Mimi, Mimi, Come down
to me and we will fly away on the wings
of song," and I think of him because then
he started to sing some fine rich romantic
song, —maybe *Some Enchanted Evening—*
while the lights came on again all over the dorm.
And now, a hundred years later, I am
in love with his gesture, with the world and its reason

well lost for love, with the "lyric imagination
asserting itself over brute fact."
I read in my text from Blake "Sooner murder
an infant in its cradle than nurse an unacted
desire," and I remember what Ezio Pinza
advised us all my high school long
"Then fly to her side and make her your own,
or all through your life you may dream all alone,"
and so sang my friend Doug to a dorm
full of girls amused, then envious, then cynical,
at last annoyed as he sang on and on
again and again, annoyed as was my roommate
when it became clearer and clearer that Mimi was not
about to come down and fly with him
anywhere. And now whatever this
means to me gets confusing, for Doug
broke off in the middle of his 7th or 8th
chorus, stopped for a moment, heard at last
the growing chorus of Southern catcalls,
turned angry, and hollered "Come on down
out of there, Mimi, or I'm going
to come on up and drag you down."
And in the silence—"Gawdamn it, Mimi—
come down," then he pulled from his pocket two
of the pistols he had gathered from our room
and began waving them in the air. By this
time, the air was filled with catcalls, Deans
of Women, sirens, and police, and Doug, though drunk,
was not so drunk that he did not sling
his pistols under a bush before anyone
quite got to him and though he spent that night
in the pokey it was for being drunk and disorderly
not for an armed assault on the girl's dorm.

It was not his first night in the hoosegow,
but it was his last as he left, by mutual
consent, the school. The night before he went,
we fought. It was the last fight of my fight-
filled youth. He would not—not fight,
so he followed me as I retreated from room
to room. At last we had at each other
in the first floor lounge, knocking over
lamps, rolling over sofas, tripping over
chairs until all of a sudden, it was enough
and we stopped. No one hurt.
No one even bruised much. I never
saw him again, but sometimes, when lecturing
on Romanticism, I wake up in the middle
of the night to the sound of my own voice
having at last found itself—and I
have been standing in front of the girl's dorm and I
have at last been singing my heart out.

An Academic Poem, or A Hero's Life

When I knew Mavis, she was the wife
of the Director of Freshman Composition. She's long
since left faculty wifing to become
a novelist, a good one, though more depressing
than I can usually stand. What made her
a hero to me happened at a party put on
by Frederick Lark, the head of the English department.

He was the worst teacher ever to be given
a festschrift. He was so bad, he was a blessing,
for the shyest, timidest, dullest, stupidest of us
could feel superior, could know that when he
said white, blue surely was in the running.

His wife Cora, however, was very sharp.
She had a Ph.D., taught English at the women's
college across town, and looked like the heavy
in *Snow White and the Seven Dwarves* in the middle
of her big scene. She would come into his class,
sit in the corner cackling and muttering under
her breath, knitting like Madame DeFarge on some
object that never got any bigger. When Lark
would say something stupid, Cora would look up,
snort, and say matter of factly, "Freddy,
you fool,"—like the time he gave the worst
single reading of a poem I've ever heard –

Haaadweeee/ butwuuurld/ eeeenuff/ and tiiime.
Thiscoi/ nyeslay/ dyeewere/ nocrime.
Weewould/ sitdow/ nyandthink/ whichwaay...

and on and interminably on until

ButatmybackIalwayshearTimeswinged
                              charyothurryingnear

his little pink mouth tripping over
itself, thin wisps of hair bobbing
above his ears, his turkey neck jutting
out further and further. "Did you catch, gentlemen,"
he asked as if in ecstasy, "Did you catch the change
of pace in the poem?"—and in the pause where he
still waited after thirty five years
for the enthusiastic response of a class—"Freddy, you fool,"
or worst of all when he was caught up
in mannerism and did a slide show of Italian
painting lecturing about the importance of the *Mona
Lisa* looking off in whatever direction
she looks off in. He had barely started
when Cora's cackling began in the corner. We listened,
caught between those two strands of discourse
until he, sitting on the last of his dull
point, looked up for comment, and she, in a seizure
of snorts and titters spluttered—"Freddy, you fool,
you've got the slide in backwards."

        Anyway, we were at this party for teaching
assistants and young faculty drinking sherry—
some nutty Amontillado—muttering
among ourselves "For the love of God, Montresor,"
as the bricks of the evening sealed us in. I
was standing next to Lenny Martin, a thin
paring of a fellow whose life was a continuous crisis.
We had been given those tiny stemmed goblets
whose tops hold about a thumb's worth.

Lark was going from glass to glass manfully
pouring. Lenny stuck out his glass.
Lark filled it. Nervous Lenny drained it
and stuck it out again and from across
a crowded room, on this enchanted evening,
Cora came flying to his side, snatched his glass
away and said—"No more good
wine for you, young man; you
get the cooking sherry." She started
for the kitchen and we get at last to the heroic part.
Mavis, about our age and standing
among the TA's offering us
a little comfort, spoke up and said,
"What the fuck do you think you're doing, Cora?"

        I know it can hardly be believed in this year
of our Lord, but that was the first time
I had ever heard the word used
in this way, not on walls, in jokes, or released
in great anger, but with the simple purity
of a necessary and moral rhetorical device.
My soul sang with it. It was like my young joy
in *Hamlet* when the Prince, gathering together
all the hatred in his heart for the old and contemptible
says to Polonius—"You are a fishmonger."

        I wish I could report that we Teaching
Assistants raised our fists as one, downed
our sherry, hurled our glasses in the fireplace,
and, bearing Mavis on our shoulders, marched
out into the night singing "Stouthearted
Men." Instead, we blanched like almonds and started
talking about the Fall, one of Lark's favorite
subjects, abandoning her as we had been taught

Adam should have abandoned Eve. Mavis's
husband finally took her away saying,
"A few of us are having this absolutely fascinating
discussion on metaphor," but a little happy ending.
Cora, startled into decency, gave Lenny back
his glass, Lark filled it, and we smiled
and smiled and went on as if nothing had happened.

I have not seen Mavis in 20 years,
but as I sit here writing this, I seem
to be in love with her. I hope her novels
become more cheerful so I can read
them, though that may be hard for someone who's been
the wife of the Director of Freshman Composition.

When this poem is adapted for the movies, I
will insist for the sake of my heart that Katherine
Hepburn star, though the young
Bette Davis was born for the part.

Making Love after Long Absence

In a room perched on top of stairs
so narrow my shoulders could not
pass through two abreast, we found
ourselves together again. I had

forgotten how light the body is.
How it surrounds us like a cloud
in which the self can drift at its ease.
Far, far away were my diaphanous

feet and half as far my hands,
and just where I ended you began,
a thousand miles off yet close as breath
the moment lungs finish their brief

rest and begin to grow again. Augustine
says body is the world's messenger to soul,
and soul gives shape again to what
she hears in her own kingdom.

So now, at the end of a day I've been
all talk, turning inward at last,
I can see you there swaying your breasts
in a grey blue lingering northern light.

Mountains Don't Have to Think about Women

Mountains don't have to think about women.
They stand, or squat, or stretch themselves out
and if the sun walks on them or the moon,
what's the difference? If the forest uses
their flank or the big-horned sheep,
so be it, though the great ones seem
to reserve a certain loneliness of head
and shoulder. If they are aware of a stream carrying
pebbles away, perhaps it is like me
on a summer's day standing at the edge of a meadow
trying not to think you are not there.

Waking from This Dream—

I am a meadow full
of flowers. You gather them up, lemon-yellow, white,
pale shades of lilac, and some of the deepest red
until your arms overflow.

I lie in bed
smiling, but sinking into myself I remember
from deeper in the night

My body is a great old forest and I am
a bear, tough-furred, big-bellied
forcing my way through the underbrush
looking
looking for something

You.

SOMETIMES YOU NEED TO LEAVE YOUR HISTORY

      Sometimes you need to leave your history
behind. So, I was shipped from the middle of 5th
grade to the middle of 6th partly because
I was bookish, but partly to escape the stronger
boys who throughout five grades
had gotten used to beating on me as I
had grown accustomed to being beaten on.
But who are you then? how much can you choose?
and what? and how do you figure on Connie?—
a girl in class whose blouse never quite
fit into her skirt so that when she went
to the blackboard to do math it pulled out
and left a triangle of bare skin maybe
three quarters of an inch thick at its widest.
Each time she was called on I sat in my
already too small chairdesk
like a wild thing caged before it had grown
into its nature, my near-sighted eyes
drawn outward to the unknowable world.
I was filled with such a pure and terrible
lust, such a longing, I ached all
over—even in my fingernails
and toenails. In all the years of my later
desirings, I have never seen flesh
that I wanted more than that thin
triangle of light brown back. What
did I want? I did not know but
at night when I lay in bed the thought of her
doing simple fractions would crack me open
and I knew there was something I had to have
that not to have it would be like death

or worse than death because I would be
alive and know I didn't have it—something
so huge, so tremendous, so
wonderful my body could not
contain it and it surrounded me like
phosphorescence. This is my soul
something wanted to say but that was far
from what I had been taught and the word
was confusing—and what to do with these feelings
more so. Even on the simplest level it was not
likely she would talk to me and if
she did, I'd have nothing to say. So,
I taught myself what we learn in the 6th
grade—that there is nothing I want that
much, that I hadn't really felt that
way, and, if I had, it was silly anyhow.
We don't have to see things even
if they're real—the cost seems small
enough—except at night, when you wake from a dream
of loss trying to think what it is
you really want, what there is at the heart
of desire and all you can remember
is, a sliver of back in the 6th grade.

Family Tree

I picture her, my great-great-great-
grandmother, say, in the long arctic summer
dusk where the light, refusing to give over,
keeps on to midnight and beyond. This woman,
bored with husband, farmers, farmer's wives,
bored with gleaming copper and bright aprons,
irritated with the neat parlor freed
only for the prison of the pastor's visit, this woman
longs for darkness. Tonight she's done her chores,
swept the kitchen, prepared the dough, milked
the cows, fed the chickens, hauled the water,
and still the light will not be quiet. So,
she says to herself,

> *Jag tror jag ska gå till skogen,*
> I think I'll go into the woods,
> *Kanhända jag möter ett troll,*
> Perhaps I'll meet a troll.

She had heard of women carried off for troll
wives. Even that would be better, to be one
of the queer ones whose eyes never rest
on things but look just beyond, whose hearts
settle at last into real stone instead
of just the pain of stone. So, she takes
off her apron, fixes her hair, and sets
off down a road that dwindles to a trail
that sneaks into a wood.

For awhile she whistles
because boys can whistle but girls must sing, but,
as the trees close over and in, the only
sound she makes is the little catch of breath
that happens at the base of the throat when the heart

beats too quickly. She shivers in her thin summer
dress as the cold lingering close to the ground
from the winter before reaches up to her
and at her. At last the trail runs
out of itself and she stands irresolute,
weight thrusting on one foot then
the other. Should she press forward where
no one has been before? Maybe it was silly,
maybe she should turn around, maybe
there are no trolls.

   She stands there
deep in wish as will can carry until
a low rumble and she turns to an upswelling
of blackness that rears and spreads its paws so wide
the rank blanket of underfur seems
a door she can enter, a dark door
which closes fiercely around as an immensity gathers
her in against itself.

   At last,
it drops back to its four paws and lumbers
off impervious to thorn or thicket or the soft
sobbing of my grandmother now just
another hurt girl sitting amidst
the ruin of her clothing able to think
of nothing else to do but go back
home and wait for the year to fall about her.

   All winter she thickened sleepily in the warm
cave of her husband's pride in having fathered.
When the lambs dropped in spring she bore
a lump all suet and hair which she licked
into a human shape. In her aftersleep
she called out—bear, and her husband said,
"*Björn*. Yes, we'll call him *Björn*."

A Story

Farley Inman—for 25 years I haven't seen you
                    or thought of you.
        Yet, here you come about me this Christmas
                        rattling your chains like Marley's ghost
                        when I try to bless or be blessed
        ready as ever to kick ass or kiss it.
                I hate your bow tie.
                I hate your high hair part.
                I hate the late adolescent grain of your cheek.
                I hate the arrogant outjutting of your ears
                        not to mention the smirk of your smile.
I called you once—no doubt you've forgotten it—you
                son of a bitch—
                "Cincinnati's Dancing Pig"
                        from the title of a popular song
                        about your hometown
                        (not top 10—maybe 15 to 20).
I must have been fending off some snotass remark of yours.
I don't want to talk to you anymore.
I'll talk to my friends out there.

        He transferred from our small-town-small
Southern Presbyterian college after pledging
Sigma Delta Tau our freshman year to Cincinnati U.
where there was a good chapter. God, I suppose
he was not unattractive in some kind of general
Midwestern clean-cut way. Farley I hate
hating you. I hate why I hate you.
I hate you because you took Roseanne
        to the Sophomore Gardenia Dance.

        Roseanne was not one of the Belles

whose legs swung like clappers
inside calf-length, gray-flannel skirts
as they strode from class to class
across town at KCW—The Kentucky College for Women.
Coopies we called Them
        (we, the horny inhabitants of Breckinridge Hall
            peckers rising high above
                the petty assault of saltpeter
                in the mashed potatoes)
or The Collection,
        The Collection at the Kentucky Corral for Wildlife.
Roseanne was beautiful,
        though shorter from hip to ankle than my taste
brought up by Betty Grable and the cartoon calendar
girls of *Esquire Magazine* said she should be.
She dwelt in the trodden way between Old Breck and the Coop
sweeping the cinders behind the counter
        of Begley's Professional Drugs, flowing
        between the mayonnaise and the meat grease
        swelling her uniform of pastel blue and dirty cream
        with such sweet swells my heart long
        in hiding now stirs for a word.
And though we could not, would not take out a town girl save
on the sly to try and get a little
of what Townies were supposed to be good for,
weekend after weekend
        we crowded 4 by 4 in 2 by 2 booths
to dine on the Saturday Surprise—
thinned out tuna plopped down amidst a tomato quadrisected
        on a leaf of lettuce too limp to last to Sunday Noon Dinner.
We watched before going on to the Saturday Movie Special
(Three Westerns
        2 starring Buck Anybody in black and white
        1 with Audie Murphy or—God Forbid—Rory Calhoun
            in Eastmancolor

6 Silly Symphonies, a Pete Smith short,
and a serial about men from Mars who from some cave
        use Miss Jane's Dude Ranch as cover)
salivating out of more glands than the salivary
as she made each sweet and Saturday Surprise
out of her sweet and Saturday self, she, Roseanne.
How could it be that it was that asshole Farley Inman
who asked her to the Sophomore Gardenia Dance?
I can't stand it. A quarter of a century
later—I can't stand it.

        Friends, you should know I was not a dancing man.
Those few I attended in high school
I spent in the cloakroom not checking coats.
The first dance that ever I danced
        I danced with Joanne Fern
        stumbling, after the movie
        (the high-class midweek Western in genuine Technicolor),
        into a social at her KCW dormitory.
        There was no out save admitting I never danced before
        which admitting I was not about to admit. Her hall
        did not even have a cloakroom not to check coats in.
She too transferred after her first year,
I don't know where—I can't believe to Cincinnati U.

        So, it was not that Farley and I were rivals.
I wasn't going to the dance with anybody.
In truth, despite my yearning, I liked women most from afar,
and did not hasten back after dancing my first dance,
and yet, I was there—I don't remember how—
perhaps with Jean Haversham—then a sophomore—
        whom I didn't go to several dances with—
        I dressing up in my father's fat old tuxedo
        she (a skinny thing, tall, a writer,
                with one eye too in love with her long nose)

arreled our bodies wait
last their owners
off leaving
each other.
nd flank to flank speak
ing language of the dumb.

donning—with amazing grace—pale green puffy
low-cut things
(Later, she grew elegant
becoming a buyer for B. Altman or
Bonwit Teller—some such place)
and we going together—but not as dates
no, never as dates.
One grand time we played basketball
all night long with the decorations
at the spiffed-up gym—dreamily trying to dribble
soft pink balloons between the dancers,
passing and shooting at the crepe-paper covered
baskets and talking and talking and talking.
Maybe that was the night when I—
fearful of an unsolicited erection
wore an athletic supporter
and my jock-strapped-in parts
grew deep and awful in their ache.
At dance's end, I could hardly walk back
from the white arches of her dorm.
Through the spring-scented, locust-silent streets
half bending, I, gathering myself to myself
around that central pain,
shuffled as if in shackles
before grave, broad-fronted houses
frowning in Southern at me.
No, that seems later—
perhaps it was just that in that time
whenever there was a place to go we all went
like my thick-necked tackle of a first roommate
also from New Jersey sitting in pained stolidity
in front of a fattening soprano singing Schubert lieder
because there was nowhere else except another Western
or the Coffee Cup Cafe which hadn't changed
its pinball machine since the original installation

in the Gold Star Summer of Nineteen-Ought-Seven.

Anyway,
        I was there,
               at the dance,
                      when Farley and Roseanne came in
               Farley smirking his smirk,
                      licking his pimpled chops
         and Roseanne in rose-red
               Roseanne in rose-red
               bare-shouldered, dark-haired,
         the tops of her breasts trembling out above
                      the crinolined carapace
         of those thrilling formals of yesteryear
         gowns modeled I learned later from top to tail
         after the breast plates of Roman Centurions.
I couldn't stand it then, I can't stand it now
that it was Farley Inman, that ass,
who took her to that dance.

        What in my smallness makes this memory bearable
is that Farley did not have the joy of her.
Discarding their dates like old corsages,
         fraternity presidents, football captains, tennis stars,
         Phi Beta Kappa candidates, veterans, yes,
         the last lorn legions of World War II
               exotic as flamingos
         surviving on the dwindling pink shrimp of the GI Bill
         cut in on him and on each other—one after the other
         a line, a conga line of tuxedoed,
               bow-tied, Adam's appled, cutter-inners
         while abandoned, unCooped Coopies
               who not long before had sipped snoot-nosed
                   lemonades
         at that very drugstore of which I've spoken

BEDTIME

Even th
and Hazl
It was Ros
      you
I think—ex
of the one g
your own par
that everyone
by emptying hi
Roseanne in rose
      you owne
        tha

I do not know what happen
    at whatever hour the
When I went back to school t
    I don't know where—c
We no longer ate at the drug st
moving on—now that someone
    to the Crossroads just outs
      having lost the salt
      we settled for the sa
      puddling over our ha

Oh Friends, the stories of my li
have long bent and cracked ben
the weight of unrescued girls.
For once, then, a happiness,
but I was not Prince Charming,
no, never charming. It was Farley In
who played that role and haunts me

If we have qu
patient as horses. At
huffy and proud set
the sweet beasts to
They turn, nuzzle,
the eloquent touch

Morning Early

        almost awake
bedclothes settled about like clouds
at the edge of summer. on the horizon
my hand floats on the warm sea of your body.
how did it get there? is it off on its own?
or has it some mysterious charter from the king,
some errand that will save all of France?
      how free it rides and easy
           on the suck and swell of your breathing.

DURING THE COLLECTION

During the collection at the First Lutheran Church,
Miss Megrim, the organist, fingers long
since fallen beneath the old German minister
goosestepping through the Gospel, scattered her music,
lost *Love Lifted Me,* and fell
twenty years into *Jesu, Joy of Man's
Desiring.* By Heavens, she got it right,
both hands together—feet too.
She who in one fifth of a century
had not hit three right notes
in succession without thanksgiving, found
herself at last played by the music, used,
(her ass firm on the bench fulcrum and fund-
amental) as she had always wanted—totally.

I say the old church danced,
got up off her knees, and gave
herself to a stately measure full of grace,
a galliard for the joy of it but with steps
befitting. Throughout this fantastic, four
men collared into choler marched down
the aisles implacable as counterpoint
making damn sure you rendered
unto Luther what was Luther's. Their feet
(feet with no nonsense, feet for flat
earths) had no ears, but who could care?

Oh lovely reader who has come this far,
sadness. It was a short church and though
I saw it try to stretch itself (though still
in dance) from porch to altar along the length

of its nave, it was, after all, only human,
and where it came to an end, it came to an end.
When the collectors had collected the collection and stood
burdens at our back, the four horsemen
of fiscal responsibility, Miss
Megrim was maybe halfway through, flushed
with the glory of accuracy and more (though God
knows that is enough) about to come
at last to that Promised Land where res-
olution seems possible. The Reverend Max
Schnell, seeing the moneys were gathered, tugged
at his chasuble—a signal which for twenty
years had set the mice of her fingers
scurrying for the hole of a C major chord
and the congregation shuffling to its feet—
but, Lord be Praised, nothing happened
but the music. Stunned, he tugged again and coughed
brought to the brink of listening (What? Ignored?
In his own house?). The third time, he matched
his tug with such a cataract of catarrh clearing
that even the pews were taken aback, and Bach,
broken, fled that place taking the dance
with him. Miss Megrim, toppled, slid
forward to the edge of her bench, teetered into
a *Do-Mi-So* and the collection went
altarward on *How Firm a Foundation.*

In Verona

      I'm sitting in a street cafe in Verona
watching 2 old Italian men watch young girls.
Across the square, the communists rally
but only the microphones have any spirit. A soft
evening sun makes a pale thin golden watery
light. One of the men is tanned and handsome
in a high-nosed Italian way. He is drinking
something the color of the air in a graceful
tall thin outcurving glass. The other is short
and squat, face scarred and warty, his clothes
catholic, body communist. He drinks beer
one after the other out of huge European
glasses. I drink Campari and soda. A young
woman walks by wearing her breasts like military
honors. This summer there are no brassieres
in Europe. I watch them shimmer then enjoy
the sway of hips as she goes her way. Though
watching her, I watch the 2 men watch her.
The tall languid one is all sighs and sadness.
The squat one's eyes burn in their comfortless
sockets.
      Three Italian women in their forties—
sisters maybe—stroll by and stop in the clearing
between us and the communists, and though they are
elegantly dressed, and though their faces
are made up most carefully, and though their smiles
flash like tourist cameras about the square,
only a glance do they win from my friends
who look hopefully up the street for a young one
then back to the comfort of their drinks.
The three women interest me—though it is true

                                            THE COMEDY OF DESIRE

the youngest one the most—and I stare at them hoping
to win one of their smiles which, though painted,
have an attractive nervous energy, but three
are too many. Besides they are out for better
game than a scruffy, middle-aged tourist.
I've come here to learn something.
Perhaps it is about getting old.

       I careen about Europe from monument
to monument in a bus filled with young people.
Though we stop regularly for diesel oil,
it is clear that Eros drives us all. The bodies
of the young quiver with it. I've watched
their eyes caught up in lust glaze over
and become as blank as the passionate marble
we so dutifully seek out each day. In Florence
we saw the David, so last night a swarm of our men
aroused by beer and wine and grappa
and singing and noise and the perpetual presence
of the other took turns at imitating
his pose in a corner of the bar lounge.
The women helped—poking a knee here,
turning slightly a wrist there, adjusting
a thigh to some secret, satisfying, remembered
angle. It is the ideal pose for the young male—
all the lines of the body, all the long
accelerating passages of energy reach towards
the sex hanging in its triple ease. The hands
are too large, capable, but the body's not
yet grown to their capacity. They are in league
with the head staring off into the distance
thinking what must be done. The message is—
the sex is the source of doing. At the museum too
I watched the watchers. The young women looked

at the David as if they could learn something,
the older ones as if they knew or longed
for something, the men with mingled envy and pride.

       The morning after—sleepless, up early
walking the streets—nothing open, no coffee,
finally an espresso bar with a sleepy-eyed girl
turning the key. Inside I stood at the counter
when 3 small dark Italians walked in, looked
at me and started to snigger. I swear I heard
Goliath among the nudges and winks. I feel
self-conscious about being outsized and middle-aged
among a busload of young Davids. They like me,
though when I walk through the streets with one
of their young women, I am the enemy, the one
they must kill before they can inherit their kingdoms.

       I think of another kind of figure—a Poseidon
or Zeus, as male and as naked as David, its arm
raised to hurl a thunderbolt or trident,
the statue in Athens, its attribute lost now
in the Adriatic. That body is filled out,
balanced, mature, muscles easy and accustomed
to such flexing. It is his will that makes
the world ring. The genitals are there too,
but part of a fuller man. We live in a time
where that energy is suspect. Our women
suspect it. We suspect it in ourselves. Maybe
we are not wrong. Yet why do I feel such loss?

       I am supposed to meet some of my young friends
by Romeo and Juliet's balcony. Instead, I think
I'll have another with my comrades here. It is good
to sit in the settling Italian sun waiting

for women to walk by, drinking bittersweet
Campari, thinking of David, thinking of how
his body grew to his hands. How do we
learn to do this, become our richest selves,
poets, kings, and lovers, and not
burn with the will's corruption?
                                    My languid
friend sighs and slips deeper into melancholy,
my angry one becomes more ferocious
in the fading light. So, body turns
towards the shadow still clinging to its old
desire. When David's blood cooled about
his kingly bones, they brought him
Abishag that young chick to look at.
I see him, as if on the wall of one
of these museums, enthroned, wrapped in a great
wool robe, holding a glass of wine
with both hands, watching her dance
not in sadness or in rage, but warmed
by the quiet presence of his longing.

        Across the square, our young bus
driver honks his impatient horn. His girl
stayed back at the pension. Time
to go. *Ciao, compadres.* I'd buy
you another, but my *lira* are running out.

A Latin Class

There were five of us, Dr. Vaughn
at his desk, the three other students right
in front of him, and me, at the back of the room,
huddled against a wall, hoping I wouldn't
be called on. It was, like Johnson's remark about
a man who got married a second time,
"A triumph of hope over experience." Once
I was asked to translate one of the poems
of Horace—the famous one with *carpe diem*
in it, "seize the day." I was seizing
the day with the aid of a 19th century
pony accurate except for an occasional flourish—
I was also practicing my dramatic presentation,
hemming and hawing. When I came to the famous phrase,
I read with gestures straight out of my
translation "Pluck the flowers of the day."
My college record has D's that I
earned. Dr. Vaughn's was a gift.

But I found myself another fall
studying Virgil for the first time in thirty
years. I loved it, read now in English,
though the image of Aeneas fleeing the burning towers
leading his son and carrying his aged father
who clutched their household gods caught
me in my middle age. I felt the weight
of my father's ghost and the urgent forward
pull of my children, and my muse
had abandoned me to my own devices and I
felt the sacked city behind, but had
no sense of a kingdom to come.

                    Despairing,
I gave up on the spirit, took to jogging, and found
my body could carry me farther than ever
I imagined when, young, I thought
of my real self as a voice rattling around
in the skull. I lifted, strained, and pushed against
strange machines. I stretched and twisted. There
was a woman I would watch play tennis—loving
that moment after the first few
games when she would break out into
a beautiful sweat, her competent body oiling
itself. From that moment she'd start to move
better, getting to balls she could not
reach before.

            How I long for such a moment
of grace, to move as easily in and with
myself as breath and not to have my
longing scattered among small untranslated
desires.

            So, graceful Virgil rose
each morning and wrote a hundred lines,
then canceled them one by one until maybe
half a phrase stood, and I see his intelligent,
wry mouth caught between smile and sigh
as he scrapes the parchment almost clean, and I hear
the steady bonk of shot after shot as a woman
practices her backhand against a wall.

LAND'S END

Where the last land drops into
the Pacific I sit and watch bulbular
clumps of weed clinging to a rock forty
feet below in the flux of the sea. On top
where the light whelms against them
they are a mustard brown green, on the bottom
deeper, darker—like the wet floor
of a mysterious forest. They stand maybe
a foot high—slender though fleshy.
The great sea swells in and over
and they give into the wash leaning
with a tuberous bend. Once in awhile a larger
wave appears and they go all
under and only the barnacle can tell what
that life is like or some small creature
clawing the bottom—and I, for a moment,
am floating on the sea, my feet somewhat
west of Hawaii and though the sea is all
around me, it is in me too
like an enormous rolling orgasm traveling
along the great Pacific Archipelago
of my legs & knees & thighs & ass
and from my waist up I am hugging
the land gasping like the first fish
flung up that tried to breathe and did
and lived to its surprise though it too died
and what's the difference and I cling to that
tiny rock swept back and forth
by the great and lovely rolling, and the sound
is the sound at the back of a throat when the breathing is fierce
though regular and the smell is the joy of an opening woman.

Again by the sea—winter now—again
I find myself looking outwards, caught
up in her vast anger. The shore today
whose very shape has been changed by the worst storm
season of a hundred years—is filled with wreckage,
weed, stone, shell, bits of torn
sea flesh, great logs and little
human-made things wrenched unrecognizable.
The waves still roll fiercely from far
out breaking over a new sandbar
then gathering up again to break once
more full upon the shore, and I think
of how on even the calmest day there
is a little shimmer against the solidness
of land, a little rolling againstness,
and I feel the ancientness of the anger
hard and tight in her belly six miles
down in the dark fold of the Mindanao Deep,
and I feel as well the old granite of my despair.

THE SNOW QUEEN

Late one night—stupid with beer, things
not well with you—leaden-eyed before
the TV—an old Danny Kaye movie—
a crumbling moment comes and you float through
that dark glass to join your soul to the soul
of that singing and dancing man—your song
a foolish song, your dance, a dance without
grace. Why are we doing this? you think,
then, a smile from the red lips of the leading lady
makes it all seem right. You think only
in the movies can someone like us win a woman
like her. Suddenly, she puts aside her mask,
and you see again your oldest enemy.

*   *   *   *

You met her first at the Paper Mill Playhouse
you, big-eyed, buttoned down in your
Sunday best—you, so caught in the story that when
she bent to kiss Kay, the boy she
carried off, you felt snow, white
snow, snow on snow, drift up the warm
summer aisle, and when her lips touched
his cheek, your cheek burned with cold
fire, and when his heart froze, something
in you turned to ice.

*   *   *   *

You were given a book of Andersen's tales
illustrated in masses of dark and white, lines

that seemed to reach so far you could not
comprehend how the page could contain
them. You read her story again and again staring
each time at her picture in profile, seated
on a throne, her body long, thin, and elegant
in the black swirlings of her robe. She burned
like a black and white flame before the gray
of the cold castle walls.

                       Years later, the book
came to you again, and you looked for the picture.
It was not there. It had never been there.
All those years it had lived in your heart, not
      in your book.

             *   *   *   *

      You tried to write about her,
casually and wittily in the rhymes of that time—

> *And in my dreams I live as Kay*
> *My heart a frozen glacier*
> *That slowly grows as every day*
> *Recedes and hardens into night.*

Now, you cannot believe it, but you did not
know what you were writing. It was as if you
thought the heart a casual organ, not needed,
in the way you can get along without a gall
bladder or a spleen, how, with a kidney gone,
      you can still piss your life away.

             *   *   *   *

      You show a friend some of these notes,

she sends a card captioned *Princess with Great*
Hopes Kissing the Local Frog and writes, "The 'Princess'
grew up to become your Snow Queen,
her lips turning to ice after having kissed
            frog after frog after frog."

                    *   *   *   *

        So she lives, the Snow Queen lives
where there is a longing for love so deep
it terrifies. For what if it will not come? What
if you are unlucky or unworthy? Out of that dread
she steps, the shadow sister of desire, the heart's
            fear of its own wanting.

                    *   *   *   *

        In one of her stories, there is a faithful one,
searching—given over to the flow of the river,
to the talk of the raven, the knife of the robber girl,
the back of the reindeer. This one has searched
since first you lost yourself. Maybe
that is your story. Maybe the one searches
for you, even here, in the frozen palace of your life.

Making Sense

Monday—a troubled 50 minutes with Peggy
trying to make sense of my life,
but I can't or it doesn't. My tongue
sits in its cage and will not move.
Why am I here? What should I say?
Then dinner with Laurie, enough pizza,
more than enough wine, and she tells
me of a poet making a pass at a conference,
which might have been all right except he didn't
remember her and she had thrown a party
for him at her house a couple of months
before. My tongue, freed from its spell,
first chirks like a sparrow then flies about
like the helpful raven in the story looking for bits
of bread. Her friend Hillary comes by.
The talk changes, still good, but different,
then the three of us go off to class
to hear Louise Glück, a wonder, beautiful
behind a flush of fever—struggling with her
illness to talk and her voice fails,
but for once I can come to the rescue having in my coat
a few cough drops, and she unfolds
the cellophane of one deliberately, puts
the freed drop in her mouth, nods at me,
and, after a moment, her voice comes singing back
along with her delight in her own speech
and she tells us that the main problem
of a writer is to diminish anxiety.

Tuesday—I'm to introduce Tranströmer
and Naomi asks if I'd like to have dinner with them.

Sure, I say, but arrive late and he
and his wife Monica and Naomi are about done
with their fish. So I order chowder
and bread which seems quick and we talk
of music and daughters and translators and poems and I
say—You look a lot like a Swedish John
Updike, and saying it I can feel my tongue
begin to roll like an old Swedish sailor's
walk. When Naomi goes to make final arrangements,
I take Tomas and Monica who has light
green eyes for a stroll around the campus
to work off dinner and wine and spring
has come even to the concrete walkways
and we feel like good friends, young
and strong, in our late 20's, say, like old
pictures of one's parents having fun.
At the church Tomas reads:

> How much we have to take on trust
> every minute we live
> in order not to drop through the earth!

and speaks of a music not for people—

> who despise themselves inside for not being murderers.

After the reading, I'm startled by a kiss on the cheek
and it's Veronica and she tells me
she's been going through the notes of a class
she once took from me and I've been on
her mind. Later, Abby and I make plans
for dinner some night. Then when I
say good night to the Transtromers, Monica says
"You are vairy Sveedish too" and, maybe

even for real, invites me to their summer sea
home, and I, pleased, smile my most Swedish smile.

   Wednesday—Up early the next morning
for a walk with Katy. We set off around
her neighborhood at a pace not much less
than a jog and I find myself wishing
I had done my stretches before I left home,
but after about a mile my breath eases
into my body and it's all right. We comment
on houses painted too dark a blue,
how cold they seem, unloving, and she knows
the good yards and shows them to me.
One is an old man's and she and he
are friends and they talk garden talk
while I lean against a fence and nod
as if I knew. She tells me as we leave
she wants to know old people—to find out
what they know—they seem to know so much—
like how to make love last. I,
older, have less faith in the wisdom produced
by simply not dying, so I grunt my most
noncommittal grunt. I take four
lemons, two in each hand, from a distant
neighbor's tree for her dessert that night,
but on the way back it starts to rain
and I shove my fists through my parka's tight sleeves
and when I give up the fruit to Katy at the door,
the top ones, the ones that rested against
the fat parts of my palms, are already squeezed.

   That afternoon I make up for a lovely while
with Judith the long quarrel that like a patient
perfect master helps us find out who

we are. Then at night I talk to Janice
and Sybil. Then Eve calls and asks if I
would like to go to the Levertov reading at Stanford.
So we meet before for sushi and saki and I
talk and talk of my days as a chauffeur's son
and she tells me of her years visiting Sweden.
I can't manipulate the raw fish
and rice with my chopsticks, so I give up
and use my fingers, licking the peppery sauce
off them after each bite. Then to the reading
and we sit behind Honor in the lecture room
and she shows us how the microphones
on the backs of the chairs work so that the usual
class can ask questions. "What are you going
to ask Denise?" she teases. "What's the name
of her orthodontist?" I reply, which seems snide
but isn't because I'm thinking of Henry
Johnson who years ago wrote a poem
about going to hear her read and falling
in love with her because of the lovely space
between her front teeth. Somehow this reading
is wrong for me, so I console myself
with old lines of hers—

> by day we are singular and often lonely

and,

> Life after life after life goes by
> without poetry, without seemliness, without love—

which sustain me as I remember how Henry
wanted to take me once to a lingerie show
where they served champagne and hors d'oeuvres
and I wouldn't go and he won't ask again

because he's dead all these years having driven
his foolish car off a foolish mountain
at a foolish hour in a foolish state just
when he had found someone to be happy with
and she had just moved into his old
house with her kids and he loved them too.
Afterwards, outside, Eve and I run into
a bunch from San Jose and I say—Eve,
this is Traise and Sandra, Eve, this
is Kathleen and Kate, Eve, this is Virginia
and Carol and all the while I'm thinking of how
once when I told Henry his poems were too skinny
and he needed to try a longer line, he arrived
at the next class with a one line poem
written on a piece of adding machine tape
50 feet long, a goddamn good 50
ft. line, and I awake to find
myself among all these women
hearing at last the loneliness of the heart
and hearing it as a source and not a terror.

LETTER TO JOHN LOGAN

Dear John,

Last night I drove to hear you read
"Spring of the Thief," the beautiful poem I've
dreamed of, and though your voice can enter
me through eye alone, it is fine to be in your
presence when body marries spirit. I love
to watch the round ruddy glow of your
face turn as, transfigured by your own
words, you look up. You need
no little cartoon floating gilded
circlet. As you read the poem I asked for,
I wept, feeling for the first time in weeks
near myself. Later I dreamed of you,
John, now I the speaker and you in the crowd.
I read stories, *exempla*, really, as a pastor
would, as if I were trying to teach
something, as if I had something to teach,
and, as sometimes happens in dreams,
I entered my own telling:

> On a hard journey at last I come to the lip
> of a great volcano, crater descending deep
> into the privacies of earth. Beneath the stillness
> a terrible energy cracks. I, the hero,
> bow, then leap into the abyss thinking
> how manly, the only cost my life.

But in the smugness of my descent, I realize
this is wrong, so I stop, come back to the reading,
look around at the rapt faces, and begin again

in a distant, muted countryside not by the sea:

> *Morning. Misty grey green.*
> *Wandering—until a woman clothed*
> *in white leads me by the hand*
> *to a secret soft damp reedy*
> *spot from where pours forth*
> *the sweet odor of nature adorning*
> *herself. The priests, though they*
> *cannot find the place, think*
> *such blessing is their doing.*
> *My beautiful guide bids me*
> *touch the ground. I kneel*
> *and find a soft round living*
> *cavity and it comes to me that I*
> *have been taken to the volcano transformed,*
> *the birthing place of the whole earth.*

John, moment by moment we father forth
in word and deed, and moment by moment we
are entered by all about us, conceive, and bear
our lives. I'll seek for the righteousness
in the heart you say perfumes these acts,
and sign this letter with great love,

Nils

LETTER TO KATY

Dear Katy,

      I was thinking of you yesterday.
I had showered and washed my hair which I do
every other day in winter because
I wear a hat and get dandruff. I
applied a touch of *Groom & Clean* on top
and a dab of *Preparation H* on bottom
and thought how much you would have liked my father.
I think a small part of my father's
smell was *Preparation H*—a strange
thing to find out and yet it makes
me feel closer to him. I've read somewhere
that tall men are prone to the affliction
my father and I occasionally share.
Humans are like columns of water in a tube—
the taller the tube, the greater the pressure at bottom
and he was tall, though not as tall as I am,
and big, as I am not. An old Swede
friend of his once told me that my father
fresh from the old country put his back
under 3 one hundred pound sacks
of flour and carried them up two flights
of steps on a bet. Al Santini, Dad's
assistant foreman when he worked the night shift,
said that one night two of his men
got into a fight and Dad picked them up
clean off the grease floor by the scruffs
of their necks and pulled them apart. I have always
pictured a percussion man separating
his cymbals. Al was full of truth and booze

and love for my father when he told me this.
Many of the men who worked for him loved him.
He was fifty-nine when he died.
At his funeral, a young man Dad
had plucked out of a flunky job to run
a trailer assembly line stuck his hand
out at me—tears in his eyes—and said
"Congratulations." He had only been
to weddings before. You've got to use whatever
language you've got. Though fifty-nine is not
tomorrow for me, it is no longer "Somewhere
Over the Rainbow" either.

                     I was thinking about
him too a couple of weeks ago
when I was off looking at a used car.
I need one and saw this ad for a 1975
CADILLAC El Dorado "fully loaded"
for under three thousand. I went
off thinking—*what the hell*. It was large,
burnt orange, and wonderfully vulgar. It had
only 40,000 miles on it
and was "cherry" as they say in these ads which damn few
things are in the world anymore including
me. I loved it. In truth,
Dad was there with me—his huge hand
giving the back of my neck an affectionate squeeze
as it used to—advising me to buy. Whenever
he triumphed he'd buy a car. Whenever he failed,
he'd buy a car. In either case, Mother,
more in touch with payments than with the promises
of the world would wail the house down. He
must have told me a thousand times as soon
as I married he'd buy a yellow convertible

Cadillac, that's how he'd say it, a yellow
convertible Cadillac, and take my mother
touring the country. Well he was dead
before I got married so that never happened,
but he did come as close as a 1957
Buick Century Convertible yellow and white
with a thin red stripe along the flow
of fender. It was a beautiful car and it came
to me. Once, when I was about to drive
to Washington to court Judith, who never
met him either, I took it through a car
wash to try and rinse away a winter's
worth of sand & salt & tar. When they turned
on the dryer, the top blew away.
I stood there stunned as strip
after strip of white canvas roof tore
and flew in the faces of the stolid Ford and Chevy
sedans moving up the line trying
to ignore one of their own dreams falling
apart. Anyway, I asked the Cadillac salesman
outright, looking him square in the eye—
"Heading straight down the freeway on a sunny
day with the wind at my back going a rock-
hard fifty-five, how many miles
per gallon would it get?" Without a blink
he said 15. That's all he could lie it up
to. Even the ghost of my father was awed at the number
of bucks it would take to drive it from the carport
to the street.

              At the poetry class the other
night Alan reminded me I owed him
a poem about an ordinary action
and then went on to assign us all a poem

that would run the risk of being sentimental.
We're not supposed to pull out of the feeling
by being either comic or ironic. Later,
he said, "An image has to fail to succeed."
He was talking about satire and the satiric
thrust—but I wonder if any image
that's any good must fail like my father's
Buick convertible in the car wash,
that success is like the victory over small
things that Rilke says makes us small.

      Ah, Katy, the only teachers are pain
and joy, and of the two, pain is the one
most continually anxious to have us learn.
But what a lovely thing to have joy
come by and lecture now and then.
A woman sitting by the door because she had
to leave at ten o'clock asked a strange
question, "How do you interpret a poem about
someone you don't know who's not from South
America?" I've been pondering on that all
this last week and I'll be damned if I know.

      Anyway, there's lots of ordinary action here
and many feelings running the risk of being
sentimental, so I'm going to type
this letter up and give Alan a copy
on Monday hoping I have managed to be neither
comic or ironic. I look forward to hearing
from you soon. With much love and many
thanks,

        Your good friend,

           Nils

Homecoming

        It's fall, night time, my old college,
a required assembly a couple of days
before my 25th reunion, 700 students, a few old
friends and teachers—*Peterson Pontificates
on Love* trumpeted the college paper
and, smiling to myself, I give them some
of the great lovely chestnuts—Catullus,
Waller, Marvell, some of my own stuff,
Corso's "Marriage," a nasty Thurber story.
Much applause—friends coming up on stage,
old teachers—we're off for a drink
at the president's house—the school no longer
dry though the county still is. Up comes
this beautiful woman, catches my eye, says
"Hi." I say, "Hi." She says, "Hi. Do you
remember me?" and in the silence—"Do you
remember me? I'm Patsy." Indeed it is.
Indeed it is. I say "Hi," kiss her on the cheek,
turn to cut off my other conversations
so we can really talk, turn back
and she's gone. "Patsy," I holler
into the cavernous auditorium, "Patsy,"
but she really is gone and to myself I say,
                "Peterson, you've done it again."

        Patsy was the girl I found for myself
my senior year after West Hill
told me I couldn't play Hamlet
because my legs were too skinny.
Long after I wrote: "that her flesh
was a slow burning hung

on lovingly articulate bones
that two decades later my bones
fall on their knees weak and dumb
at the thought of her knees unclenching."
Now, lost again—and all through the president's
bourbon and branchwater my thoughts swirled
with her—sure—the long lovely nights
with blanket and beer on a ledge looking out
at Lake Harrington but maybe even more
the years after my first loss when fate
would take me through Cincinnati,
over the river, through Covington, and right on by
the curving drive which led to her lovely house
set on its small rise and my heart
                    would squeeze into itself.

        Next day to the alumni office for address
and phone number—she lives in Lexington—not far,
divorced—has a couple of sons—one enrolled
here—I call—no answer—and later—no answer
maybe she's in town for the Homecoming
maybe she's here, maybe she's there.
I look in both places. I call—no answer,
the next morning—5:30 A.M.—I call
no answer. All through the big game
I pace the stands even on the side of our dreaded
rival not caring who won or lost, but no
Patsy. Game over. Plane out tomorrow. Dance
at the club after cocktails at my classmate's
now a judge and all irredeemable.
Into the judge's pantry for a last call,
by now I know the number—dial—and yes
she answers and yes she says Hi and no, she'd
been out fox hunting when I called so early

and yes she's free for dinner. So I abandon my
goodbyes to my good buddies and dances
with many a girl I longed for long ago
and sneak out the back way and up the old road
                    I'd driven so often on the liquor run.

            Old house, wide porch, October moon,
nervous me, door opens, and there she is,
my old girl still, but a woman now
and even more beautiful. And yes, we both
preferred Martinis, and yes she still smoked,
and yes, the big oil hanging above
the long stairs belonged to a former poet
laureate of Kentucky who once owned the house,
and yes it was nice to see me again too.
And then we began to talk—each with a quarter
of a century of life to give the other,
she, her tall strong sons, I, my lovely
daughters, she her trip to Japan just
after we'd broken up, I, my unexpected
love of Sweden, she the wife of a premed,
I a graduate student, and no she didn't
have my old fraternity pin, she thought
she'd given it back and the black purse I'd bought
at Saks—long since worn. I still had
the silver cigarette lighter, though I no longer
carried it, and a book—"The Kentucky Story,"
given to me so I wouldn't forget. She had lost
one of the jade earrings I had blown a week's
salary on but she'd had the other made
into a ring, yes, the one she was wearing,
and the hard times—her divorce,
my separation. By now we're at dinner,
too much bloody meat and too little

anything else, and a New York wine
made out of red ink and sugar, yet all sang
on the tongue, and one of her sons worked there—
yes, he was tall and handsome, and gave me
his hand and half a raised eyebrow—then back
to her place for an after-dinner drink
in front of a warm coal fire burning
vermilion and black in an old metal stove
and talk while the hours fled with the flown years.
What the young offer each other
is the marvelous future, all that can happen,
all that will be. Older, suspicious
of promises, we learn to offer what we have lived.
It is a smaller, harder gift, yet beautiful like fact.

        When it was at last time to go, we held
each other long and hard, maybe even harder
than all those nights out at the lake,
as if somehow that would help us with who
we were, as if we could bind the years,
our separate lives and those fine lives
linked with ours and grown out of ours
together—in our arms, then off I went
into the night drunk on nothing I had swallowed.

        We wrote for awhile and I thought it was she
that stopped, but, looking through an old notebook,
I found my last letter unstamped, unmailed
and thought, Peterson, you've done it again. But
it's Valentine's Day and I'm preparing to pontificate
on love again and all this comes flooding back,
so, I begin —

        "Hi. Do you remember me? I'm Nils."

A Journey

One day peering down at the earth, we feel a sudden longing, so we set off down the stairs to the great secret door where the body accepts us and we float solemnly past the lungs and the heart singing its sad song to itself.

Pulled downward by the dense gravity of the genitals we wonder if they are where we are meant to go, but hear a deeper call beyond the great forking—and which leg will be the one we travel by?—the right, for all our lifetimes when we rose from our chairs have we not set off with the left, while the right, diffident, hung back bearing the weight and thrust of our leaving? So, we clamber down the right thighbone, beyond the knee, and enter the far outpost of the foot.

Then we set about learning to dance before the forest, before the dark, dark forest.

Thanks

I wish to thank the editors of *San Jose Studies* and the members of The San Jose Center for Poetry and Literature for their continual support.

I wish to thank Ed Kessler, Naomi Clark, and Abby Niebauer for good talk, and my other teachers in the classroom and out of it.

I wish to thank Tomas Tranströmer for his lines on page 55, and to Robert Bly for his translation of them.

I wish particularly to thank the editors of this volume, Andrew Dick and Robert Bly.

Nils Peterson

❃

About the Poet

Nils Peterson was born in Plainfield, New Jersey, and has lived most of his adult life in California, where he teaches Creative Writing and Shakespeare at San Jose State University. He is a graduate of Centre College in Kentucky and did his graduate work at Rutgers University. He is married to Judith Peterson, a therapist in private practice, and is the father of two daughters, Erika and Cecily. This is his first full-length collection of poems, but he has published earlier a chapbook, *Here Is No Ordinary Rejoicing.* He is well-loved in San Jose, especially for his readings of love poems from all over the world which he gives in downtown San Jose every Valentine's Day.